OUR JOURNEY

In all I've tried to do, I tried to walk with you
I tried to live with you and by your rules
At times I am rocked
Swayed
Confused
Want and need to leave you
But I am still with you

Still walking a lonely and hard road with you

Life comes and many give it away
Choose death over life
Now their journey must end because death was their good and true choice; stay.

And although the road is rough and tough with me

Weary
Deadly
I have to journey on my way and shed the pain.

I have to live free
Embrace true freedom without restrictions
Fear
Woes
Pain

Thus you Lovey are more than my good and true Sheppard despite me wanting and needing to leave you.

The journey is long, and I did walk in the valley of the shadow of death; I did fear evil at times, but you were with me; my true way.

Many storms came and went but you were and still are my protector, rod and more than staff that protects me.

You are my comforter, rock of more than ages because you do comfort me. You are my way and light because I know the true light in the darkness and that true light is you.

And as the year 2015 comes to a close, I close with you hand in hand this fiscal year and begin anew.

I close the year in truth and true love between me and you, my good and true family, children, the good and true seeds you've given me, the good and true universe,

OUR JOURNEY/MY ANGER

good and true spirits of the spiritual realm, the good and true angels of above and below, the good and true earth and my good and true mother, Miss Peggy, Rosalind Rosetta Morgan as well as my good and true ancestors that are before me. Yes the flesh is no more but the good and true spirit live on.

To my great grandmother; I will truly not forget you because despite it all you were there with me when I journeyed home before Lovey deemed Jamaica unclean.

As for you my grandmother, there is much to be said, and I wish you the best despite you truly not loving me.

I cannot and will not hold a grudge. I release me from my pain and suffering when it comes to you. You are gone now but will not be forgotten. I forgive you as I forgive myself. Walk good and well because my dark road and path has and have come to an end. I release my demons and lock them in hell because true darkness isn't about pain and holding on to the past. It's about the good light that is within you; your true heart and purity of soul and spirit. I know the truth and it's good and well to know and do the truth. So as I let go of my past and all that hurt me, I embrace true life and the truth of you and me; Lovey. I have to move forward without the hurt and pain; therefore Lovey, let 2016 be our true and good beginning that is filled with joy, true joy and true peace, true happiness, good and true health and wealth; prosperity.

OUR JOURNEY/MY ANGER

Let our words be kind to each other.
Let our world be pure and clean.
Let us not hurt each other or keep each other lonely.

Let true good and clean goodness surround us always so that we can continue to give in truth, true goodness; true peace and prosperity.

Sins are there and we've all sinned including me, thus we have our day and you Lovey; Good God and Allelujah have your true day. Never leave me confused and lonely again because the worst is over and I truly want and need to live in true peace and harmony with you here on earth. So as the year closes, help me to clean up earth; my life, the good and true life of others including you Lovey in a good and true way.

All the clutter and nastiness in earth and in my home that need to go; let it and or them leave or go in true peace infinitely and indefinitely more than forever ever without end.

The time of evil has expired; so let death take their people and go. Earth can no longer be the home of the devil and all that is wicked and evil; nasty.

Earth and the universe including the spiritual realm must come clean and let go all that ails them; cause them pain; hurt. It won't be easy but in order to do this; clean our surroundings, all that is wicked and evil must go never to ever return.

OUR JOURNEY/MY ANGER

You have the sinful records of man including my sin record. I will not take myself out of this because I too have sinned against you. Yes you asked me to write you a book twice and I've written and still writing, but I cannot be unjust and exclude me out of all of this. Like I've said, I too have sinned thus hurting you as well.

I am not a saint but my true and good heart is pure and clean towards you and in truth, I am truly tired of the evil and wickedness that is happening here on earth. Man to man is truly unjust; thus my anger will explode in this book. You know this thus the title above.

Lovey you are my Allelujah of goodness and truth always. You are a part of my good and true life and despite me wanting and needing to leave you and slowly leaving you; do continue to be there for me despite it all.

<u>I truly do not want or need another god; I just can't take the pain and loneliness of my life anymore. I cannot take any more violence here on earth. The pain is too great and in truth; I can no longer see the earth suffer because of the wickedness of man; us humans. She deserves better; so I am pleading her cause and case with you. Truly let earth; the good earth find hope, true peace and rest from all the wickedness and evil that we as humans do in her. She needs this Lovey come on now.</u>

I truly cannot cheat on you with another god because despite my complaints and nagging; you are in the storms with me and as of late you've been comforting me.

I need true peace and cleanliness in my life Lovey and I cannot have it in an environment that I am truly not happy in. So I have to slowly let go of you because you are truly not hearing and or listening to me.

Like Earth and Mother Africa, I am tired. Tired of seeing death's children destroy and kill it all because of vanity; greed.

I am tired of my health and financial woes.

Tired of seeing death walk and talk; well death does not talk much; take at will.

Lovey humans made their choice of death, so why don't they leave earth and go?

Why do they have to stay?

Why do we have to hold on and endure in a planet that is not safe anymore?

Why do we have to struggle so hard to find you and bring you back?

Why even let good reside next to wicked and evil people and spirits?

OUR JOURNEY/MY ANGER

Lovey, why can't we build a true home for our self here on earth or somewhere in the universe that is void of all wicked and evil people and spirit; sin; a world where sin and evil cannot infiltrate or come in?

Ah Lovey, let your true goodness and mercy fill me with joy and true peace; harmony and true giving all the days of my life so that we can be together with our good and true people more than forevermore.

Oh Lovey let the words in this book move you to do that which is right, good and true, just for all who are good and true; all who are fed up of the fighting and war; strife and pain, hardship and hardships of this life here on earth and in the spiritual realm and universe.

Let our sufferings and hardship come to an end as of the ending of this fiscal and financial year which is December 31, 2015.

Yes I know our time is not like your time and earthly time must catch up to your time. So I am asking you Lovey with a true and pure heart, let our time, my time and your time unify as one in truth and true peace; good and true, pure and wholesome harmony.

Michelle
December 08, 2015

Oh Lovey is this the end of our journey?

No, it isn't. I'm just bored and I truly can't get to sleep.

Want to eat something and drink a cup of coffee but the adverse reaction of getting a heartburn I truly do not want or need.

Can't drink coffee after a certain time and or hour and I don't have any Jamaican chocolate to make tea.

Ah what a bummer.

Ah Lovey, this world has become dangerous to live in.

You can't trust anyone, hence there is truly no clean living here on earth.

Ah Lovey, I don't know, truly don't know.

Michelle
December 02, 2015

Ah Lovey if only we could escape to an island or country in the sun.

If only my life wasn't this hard financially; physically and spiritually.

If only I could get away and eat jelly coconut each and every day.

If only I could have roast breadfruit, mangoes, fried plantain, cassava, carrots, cabbage, beans, papaya, yellow yam, soft yam and more to eat from clean hands and a clean, good and pure heart.

Oh Lovey if only, truly if only.

Michelle
December 02, 2015

Freedom
Wow
What is freedom?

Is it free will?
A new beginning
The race or a race in time

What is freedom to me may not be freedom to you. So what is freedom truly and really?

What is freedom to you?
Is it walking naked in the streets?

Is it having fun?
Clubbing
Taking vacations in the sun

Is it doing what you want and need to do without restrictions and constraints; a prison wall?

Come on tell me; what is freedom to you?

It is a great getaway?
Winning the lottery

Is it financial freedom to do what you want when you want; or is it, just lounging around doing absolutely nothing?

Michelle

OUR JOURNEY/MY ANGER

I need your sweet embrace
I need your truth
True love
Desire

But in all that I need and want, do I truly have you?
Could you truly give all of you to me?
Could you cherish me for who I am?
Could you define me?
Complete me in a positive and true way?

Could you be my world?
My total and absolute freedom?
Desire

Could you be my good and true fruit tree?
Fruits

Could you be my lifelong partner; host?
Most

Could I satisfy you and your desires completely more than forever ever without end?

Are you a pleaser or are you a user and abuser?
Are you genuine?
My true and perfect fine wine?

Are you a give and a receiver?

Are you strong or weak?

OUR JOURNEY/MY ANGER

A fraud?
Fake

Are you a mover and a shaker?

Are you smooth like a smoothie?

Are you sweet or are you sour?

Are you truly free?
My journey
Heart's true desire

Are you meek?
Friendly
A tamed lion

What are you?
Are you me?
You
Whatever.

Michelle

Ah Lovey could you follow my true heart and be with me forever ever in goodness and in truth?

Couldn't you and my Mother be my good and true desire?

Wait, you both are already.

See Lovey, I am bored and I truly do not know what to write.

Maybe another day, but not someday; I'm just bored.

Lovey, I so need to be in the sun soaking up all the vitamin D I can get.

Oh Lovey, if only I had the money. Trust me I would so not spend Christmas or my birthday and your day here.

I would fly away to someplace warm so that we could be together as a family.

So yes, life sucks with me financially Lovey.

Michelle
December 02, 2015

Bored bored bored. Yes I am bored. Don't know who to nag; so I am nagging my readers again with my boredom.

I so can't take or stand winter.

Man do I ever need to go for a walk right about now but can't because it's cold outside.

Have no friends to call or hit up on the telephone. No, I so don't want to talk to anyone or hear anyone's problems

I'm just bored, totally bored.

Damn my life is boring and I so hate winter.

Yes the true prisoner life because my body truly cannot stand the cold; can't take anymore winters.

Michelle
December 02, 2015

OUR JOURNEY/MY ANGER

Mess mess mess
What a mess

It's cold and my body is breaking down
Too cold to do anything

I am but a prisoner of the cold
Walls closing in on me because it's too cold
I feel like I am in a jailhouse
Caged due to the cold

I am bound
Damn where is the key
Where is the key
Where is the key

I am looking
Searching
Can't find

Lovey where is the key
Why can't I find the key to escape this cold indefinitely?

Why Lovey
Why

Send me the key
Give me the key
The key
The key
Aaaah

Where's the key?
Where's the key?
The key

I am going crazy
No not crazy
Yes crazy

Lovey where's the key
Where's the key

Why leave me prisoner in the cold?
Why neglect and abandon me?

Loveeeeeeey, where's the key
The key
I am searching
Why can't I find the key?

Loveeeeeeey, where's the key?
The key
The key

Loveeeeeeeey, where are you?
Where's the key?
Aaaaah the key.

Michelle
December 08, 2015

Lovey, there is so much more to life that I truly do not know. So as we journey beyond the stars and this universe, let true truth be known.

We say man cannot live by bread alone, but what is bread to man?

In all we need, we need life; water because water maintains and sustains us all including this earth.

We need water to clean not just self but the spirit.

We need water to grow our food, keep our body and spirit nourished; hydrated; clean.

So Lovey what say you?

The journey of all who are wicked and evil must come to an end. Evil and or negative forces cannot continue to dominate and control including contaminate the life and lives of the good of this earth any longer.

Tell me something Lovey, how can we journey on in truth given the current status of earth due to sin and the unclean ways of humans and animals?

Have we as humans not made life unclean and void of all truth here on earth?

How could you as Lovey and Good God and Allelujah want a home in a dirty planet that is infested with dirty and wicked people?

Lovey you are good and true, but when does all become clean and whole again all around?

<u>Lovey, if we start off dirty with you, will we not remain dirty in the end?</u>

CAN THE BEGINNING BECOME CLEAN IF WE HAVE DIRTIED IT?

No it cannot. So why do you let us as humans dirty you and this earth including the universe and spiritual realm?

In order for you to remain clean you have to start off clean. Thus marriages truly do not work because neither party was clean from the get go. So because of our unclean nature, we pollute all including others. We go from one relationship to the next with the same dirty self and continue on with the lies we say we left behind.

And no, one party cannot be truthful and the next a liar. It will not work because the liar makes the truthful one unclean; thus both become unclean; dirty.

Clean cannot live with dirt because **<u>ABSOLUTELY NO ONE CAN MAKE DIRT CLEAN. IT IS INFINITELY AND INDEFINITELY IMPOSSIBLE.</u>**

Say it so I can school you. Take up the dirt of the earth and make it clean if you can. Better yet, take a white sock, wear it for a day or two, wash it; now tell me if that sock is as clean as the day you bought it and or took it out of the package?

No amount of bleach, soap and or peroxide including baking soda can make that sock brand new. So no, if you start out in lies, you cannot end in truth because that lie will always follow you. Thus our sins follow us everywhere we go.

But but.

There are no but buts. Sins are death. SO DEATH FOLLOW US EACH AND EVERY DAY, EVERY SECOND AND NANA SECOND. WE CANNOT GET RID OF DEATH ONCE WE'VE SINNED AND THIS DEPENDS ON THE SIN.

Some sins you can make amends and or atonement for, but some sins are automatic death. Thus I've just told you, death follows you everywhere you go. No one can run from death because death is always by your side even when you are sleeping; showering.

DEATH IS GUARANTEED FOR BILLIONS. THUS LIFE IS NOT GUARANTEED FOR THE WICKED AND EVIL. BILLIONS DID NOT MAKE LIFE THEIR GUARANTOR; TRUE CHOICE.

Michelle

MY ANGER

Ah anger is a bitch
The yelling
Raised blood pressure
The foul language
Hurtful words
Fist fights

The turned backs
Unspoken words
Broken marriages
Relationships
Family
Anger
Rage

Infidelity turns to pain; more anger, hurt

Burst blood vessels
Clenched fists
Blood
Gore
Fight
Slaughter
War

We all get angry for different reasons in different seasons. The pain come and go and we move on. Some rage on causing war; total destruction; annihilation.

In this section of this book I will get angry; release that which is pent up. I will be harsh and I will fear nothing because there is nothing to fear. No one can fear the truth because when all is said and done, the truth must stand; outlast all the tests of time.

In life we say truth is everlasting life, but why are we not telling the truth. Lies cannot save us but yet; we hang on to lies and conceal the truth and this is sad. You may not like me. Hell you might just hate and loathe me, but in truth; I truly don't give a damn. As humans we cannot say we love but yet live by lies. Lies do not rain down from God, so why do we believe in lies and tell lies?

Michelle

How can I walk and talk with you Lovey when men and women defy you?

How can earth be free and clean when men and women including children change their sex at will to reflect the other sex?

Lovey, How?

You know what, let me truly forget it because our journey is slowly coming to a halt and this is truly fine by and with me.

The disgusting lifestyles of humans on this earth is truly getting to me and you are the root cause of it all Lovey.

You are to blame because you permit crap like this to happen.

Mother Earth too is to blame because she sit idly by and let humans contaminate and destroy her in the worst of ways.

Michelle
December 07, 2015

Am I angry Lovey?

You damned right I am angry.

Why Lovey?
Why?

Now do you see why I want to truly leave you?

You don't care about my well being or the well being of your good and true people.

How the hell can you and Mother Earth allow men and women including children to go under the knife and change the sex of their birth including their birth certificate to falsify self?

Wow

That's all I got to say; thus justice is truly blind; flawed for real.

Michelle
December 07, 2015

OUR JOURNEY/MY ANGER

I want to be free
Want to walk naked as the day I was born

Want to feel the wind beneath me; all around me

Yes I want to be free
Free to walk
Run
Roam
Get angry

Freedom I cry
Freedom I cry

Need to be free
Free from the negative forces of earth and nature
Free from the shackles and chains of man; humanity

I need to be free
Free from racial divide
Hatred
Fear
War

I want to be free
Free to walk
Talk
Dress the way I want to
Marry the clean and good mate I need and want to

Someone that is honest with a good and pure heart

I want and need to be free
Free from the countries that promote it things isms.

I need and want to be free
Free from societies that condone and shelter the lies of it things; transgender garbage that pollute and contaminate this earth.

I want and need to be free
Free from a society and societies that promote sin and transgender it things.

How can a man that was born a male or female change his or her sex including birth certificate to reflect another sex when they were not born that way? Hence I say there is no true justice in this world.

Lovey and Mother Earth promote and condone too much damned slackness.

Thus there is truly no freedom on earth in the truest of sense. Therefore, the justice system of man is flawed making Superman; the Supreme Being a fake and more than flawed, a fraud.

Michelle
December 07, 2015

What a life when the wicked and evil of this earth can do as they damned well please.

What a life when the wicked and evil of this earth can disobey the laws of life each and every day and get away with it.

So tell me, where is the justice for life and all the good people in life?

Yes I am angry.

Angry at God.

Angry at Death.

Angry at the Universe and Earth for letting this shit happen over and over again.

Thus Earth has and have become a bitch nigger for the niggers of this world; earth globally.

Humans condemn and destroy her and there isn't a damned thing she can do about it.

Michelle Jean
December 07, 2015

2015 comes to a close and I am not sorry the year is done.

Too much heartache and pain, anger and nastiness.

Yes I know I should not be angry at Lovey but I am.

Good riddens 2015.

Hello 2016.

Let's hope you come in with a bang and bring loads of prosperity and goodness for me and the good people of this earth.

Michelle
December 07, 2015

Wrote about J. Capri in my book REAL SITUATION and I read she was speeding and she lost control of her car. I also read the doctors had given her the green light to make a full recovery. Now the family is doing an autopsy to see if disease and or infection was a factor in her death. Also read the hospital had her in an induced coma before she died.

Now di anger a guh spew because if it's the same University Hospital that the 18 babies were murdered due to infection and negligence on the hospitals part; I truly hope hell hath no fury when it comes to this hospital. An nuh baddy betta tell mi no claate how Jamaica's hospitals are. I bleeping know how they are. Human life is not counted nor are people treated with dignity and care. I've experience this first hand with this ghetto belly wey call harself a bleeping nurse.

How the fuck can doctors and hospital staff know the severity of the problem at University Hospital and kept the hospital open? Quarantine the fucking hospital until you have the virus and or disease under control so that others don't come in contact with it; this virus and or disease.

Eighteen fucking babies died and NEITHER DOCTOR NOR THE MINISTER OF HEALTH HAVE AND HAS BEEN FIRED AND HELD ACCOUNTABLE FOR NEGLIGENCE AND MASS MURDER.

DOWN TO THE FUCKING PRIME MINISTER SHOULD BE FIRED BECAUSE SHE HAS NO COMPETENCE AND OR WORTH WHEN IT COMES TO HER PEOPLE. And you the Jamaican public and people are fucking morons that run behind these low life and garbage each and every election anna support dem.

<u>Unnu run lackka fucking idiots while they have you starving and hungry. Grow the fuck up and wake the fuck up and have some fucking ambition for self.</u>

<u>Every day unnu complain bout dem an as soon as election time come unnu come in lackka wharf dawg a follow dem anna sniff dem backside fi likkle food.</u>

WHAT THE FUCK YOU VOTE INTO OFFICE TO REPRESENT YOU IS WHAT YOU FUCKING GET. IF A MAN HAS NO RESPECT FOR YOU, HE CANNOT AND WILL NEVER EVER TAKE CARE OF YOU; NOR WILL HE OR SHE RESPECT YOU.

THUS BLACK PEOPLE HAVE NO WORTH GLOBALLY BECAUSE WI TOO FUCKING FOOL FOOL.

Eeee cum eeene like when idiocy was being given out the black race went back in line time and time again.

WE FUCKING STRESS HOW WE ARE CREATORS AND BUILDERS AND HOW WE CREATED THIS WORLD AND UNIVERSE, BUT I ASK YOU; GIVEN THE CURRENT SITUATION OF BLACKS GLOBALLY, WHAT THE FUCK DID WE CREATE; BUILD?

WHAT DID WE CREATE?

OH, WE CREATED STUPIDITY AND IGNORANCE.

That's all we got. Fuck the lots of you. None of you created a damned thing; nothing. And don't you dare tell me about we were enslaved and all that the black man and woman created was taken and or stolen from them. We as blacks could not put our names on our inventions. <u>Bitches I know that, but I want to vent my way to get you to fucking think and do a lot better come 2016 and beyond if the black race is to survive the brutal harvest that is coming.</u>

That fucking moron that runs Jamaica right now, man if I could create a hell for her right now I would but I can't.

Judgment is not mine; thus all I have is my anger.

Eighteen babies died people. Eighteen fucking children; babies died and no one has been held accountable for these murders. No Doctor, no Minister of Health, no Prime Minister. Now if the lab result come back for J. Capri and find she contracted a virus and or disease; what the hell are they going to tell me and the world?

Now I ask you, **HOW MUCH MORE BABIES AND PEOPLE DIED AT THIS HOSPITAL THAT THEY ARE COVERING UP?**

HOW MUCH MORE BECAUSE BLACK LIVES DO NOT MATTER GLOBALLY; NOR DOES IT MATTER WITHIN OUR OWN FUCKING WUTLESS RACE; COMMUNITY.

Wi fuck an ha pickney wuss dan fucking cockroach and dogs and can't tek care a dem. Yes I am on a tirade right now because I am so fucking disappointed in my own black people right now.

When do we fucking wake up and start respecting self as individuals as well as a race and community?

I should not have to write books of anger like this to get us to fucking wake up from the deep sleep we are in. We cannot say <u>**BLACK LIVES MATTER AND OUR CHILDREN AND OR PEOPLE ARE BEHIND BARS AND LIVE IN COMMUNITIES THAT ARE NOT SUITABLE TO LIVE IN.**</u>

WHY SHOULD WE BE PORTRAYED AS SCAVENGERS THAT LIVE IN RAT INFESTED HELL HOLES?

We created it all, but yet as creators; we fell from grace and live as beggars and thieves, rapists and murderers.

SO NOW I ASK YOU:

WHEN DOES BLACK LIVES MATTER?

WHEN?

Why should people and babies have to die due to negligence?

Lovey lives were lost and it's as if no one truly gives a damn in Jamaica. It's as if this is the norm. <u>**Death is a gang Lovey because death kills brutally at the hands of the wicked and evil; the don't care of society.**</u> Thus death kills by any means necessary. Malcolm X

You gave us life and we destroy it; then turn around and say you are going to send us a saving grace.

How the hell can you Lovey send a saving grace for murderers, liars and thieves; sinners that think they are above the law?

<u>EIGHTEEN BABIES IS MASS MURDER LOVEY COME ON NOW.</u> Frigging mass murder and you are okay with this?

What chance did those babies have to life?

Why is the wicked and evil still living?

Why isn't their wickedness being turned back on them Lovey?

Do you favour the wicked and evil over good and true life? Come on now

WHERE IN YOUR HANDBOOK OR MANUAL DOES IT SAY; THE WICKED AND EVIL GO FREE FOR ALL THE WICKEDNESS AND EVIL THEY HAVE DONE HERE ON EARTH?

WHY SENTENCE US TO DEATH WITH THESE VILE AND EVIL PEOPLE?

Why should the good spirits of the spiritual realm walk amongst them; the wicked and evil; defiled of this earth and universe including the spiritual realm?

NOW TELL ME THIS LOVEY, WHY IS THE LAWS OF MEN DIFFERENT FOR DOCTORS, LAWYERS, CIVILIANS, THE CLERGY AND POLITICIANS INCLUDING BUSINESS MEN AND WOMEN?

Is earth the planet of death?

So if earth is the planet of death and doom, why are your people which is our good and true people trapped here?

Evil cannot be reformed, so what are we doing on this planet?

Humans care not who and what they kill, so why let evil and wicked humans; men and women have dominion over this earth?

Cleanliness is not in the hearts of man; humans, so why let women lay with them?

Yes you forbade Eve (Evening) from lying with him according to man's nasty book, but she did anyway. But Lovey, the lie goes further back; further than Adam and Eve. So I ask you this, <u>**if black is the foundation of life, why is there so much evil and wickedness on earth and in the universe?**</u> *Yes I felt peace; true peace when I saw the birth of life, but why taint life? I mean, why let humans taint life?*

Why let us in if we were going to destroy and kill life like this?

Why not let life; good and true life truly live?

I don't know Lovey because the pressure want to start rising in my head.

Look at the cost of life Lovey?

Now tell me, where is the true truth in you?

We are cut off from you and exiled on a planet that has no good and true laws when it comes to life. Men create unfair laws globally; thus humans are not clean, nor are they truly fair in anything that they do. Thus we are the true children of Cain because according to man's nasty book; he was a stingy bitch and murderer.

Yes we see this each and every day.

And yes we are the ones to allow evil in our lives, but why can't we as humans see that men are truly no good?

I mean look at the course of history Lovey and tell me why do men have to fight and kill?

Why do they have to dominate and control? And if they cannot dominate and control they kill; why?

Why do men not value life?

Are they blind and ignorant to life Lovey?

No, that's a stupid question. They are blind and ignorant to life. Thus men strive for control, domination and power.

Women are classed and blamed for a lot of things, but yet you see and know this and do nothing about it. We do not go out there and wage war because to many of us; **_LIFE IS KEY AND IT IS VALUED ABOVE ALL THAT IS WICKED AND EVIL._**

Its like men have to be the head of everything.

They have to dictate, but yet they hold no place with you Lovey. All your good and true chosen are females not males.

Females carry life for you and not males, but yet the world cannot see this. The world and or humans of this world truly do not want or need to know this.

We truly cannot live life Lovey because we truly do not know life, nor do we want to either. So how can you save nations globally when nations truly do not know you or value you and your laws?

So yes, you are powerless Lovey because you cannot change the lives of men for the better; nor do men and women including children want to change their lives for the better. You Lovey are locked out of earth due to the sins and evils of men women and children. So yes, you are truly powerless and without justice all around.

You too have become the slave and prisoner of men; humans because in truth, <u>HUMANS DICTATE TO YOU AND THERE ISN'T A DAMNED THING YOU CAN DO ABOUT IT.</u> HUMANS PLAYED YOU IN THEIR LITTLE NASTY BOOK AND WON BECAUSE HUMANS WORSHIP AND PRAISE DEATH AND FORGOT ABOUT LIFE; YOU.

YOU WERE THE PAWN FOR HUMANS BECAUSE WE AS HUMANS LOCK YOU OUT OF YOUR OWN CREATION; THIS EARTH.

Yes I know humans cannot win against you Lovey, but I have to say this and do this to get you to truly think and see the real situation of this earth. Look at it, do many not think you do not exist?

Do many not say they have the key to you whist deceiving millions and billions?

Do many not use you as their free ride to capture the souls and spirit of millions and billions whilst locking them in hell infinitely and indefinitely for time times time? Come on now

So were you not the pawn and scapegoat for many men and women in earth's so called society? So tell me

Lovey, what makes you so powerful on earth when death owns you; well own this earth and the people of this earth?

Earth is also powerless because she cannot fully get rid of evil and she cannot rotate counter clockwise and change her gravitational pull to eliminate all who are wicked and evil; sinful.

She knows not the negative pull of evil; thus she cannot latch on to this negative source and eliminate it from her more than infinitely and indefinitely without end more than forever ever. Therefore, the wicked and evil will forever have a place in earth to do their evil and nastiness.

The Universe is also powerless Lovey because he cannot get rid of evil. Evil spreads and evil is consuming the universe just as evil is consuming and killing earth.

Death rules Lovey thus millions are born to death each and every fiscal year. So tell me, what truly say you?

Come on Lovey, you've got no place with humans.

Which human being truly want and need to know you?

Yes the calm in my dream world is truly here.

There is a different feel this December and I truly don't know why.

I have to wonder if this is truly the calm before the storm and all hell is going to break loose in 2016.

Wow, saw the map of the world at least countries of the world recently. I can't remember which lands in the Caribbean and Africa that were being shown to me. I so can't remember if these lands were disobedient lands, but for sure Jamaica was one of them. Oh well this is life I guess.

Wow people I have to ask, **_HAVE YOU EVER HAD A SLEEP IN A SLEEP EXPERIENCE?_**

I know this is something truly new, well for me it is. It's like I was sleeping in a sleep. Therefore I call it sleep in a sleep. It's like one of the best sleep you've ever had. There is truly nothing weird about this sleep but the sleep is good.

Hey maybe it's me because I am the true weird one.

Dreamt about Konshens the reggae artist. Dreamt he had a baby but the baby was ugly and of two tone. The baby had a black patch in its face and the rest of the body of the baby was light skinned and or of a lighter hue. He Konshens was happy that he had a baby. So he gave me the baby to hold. People, di ole mi ole di pickney, mi almose drop di pickney to how hebby di baby is. **_Mi sey one piece a baby weight tek mi yu si._** Di weight a di baby come eene like dead weight to yass. All in all; I did not drop the baby. I was about to tell

Konshens di baby nuh look like him an a nuh fi him pickney but I didn't get a chance to. But man was Konshens ever happy. The moral of the dream was **_WHAT DO NOT CONCERN YOU LEAVE IT ALONE._** So come 2016, what do not truly concern me I am going to have to truly leave it alone. No I can't. You all know me when it comes to injustice. I truly cannot stand injustice so I will not keep my mouth shut in these books. The truth need to be told; thus Lovey gave me a good and true voice and I am going to use it. Yes I see certain things and some people will want to muzzle me, but no one can muzzle the truth. The truth cannot lie nor will it lie for anyone come on now. So no, death cannot muzzle me because I do not work for death. I live for life and life is my good and true choice. So I have to truly help good and true life.

No one should have to stand for injustice and we as humans need to start respecting our self individually.

We have life and were given life and I truly do not know and or comprehend why we would hand our life over to wicked and evil people that has no one's best interest at heart.

No people; truly look into your life and look at the environment you live in. We elect men and women and call them government officials and so called pastors and what have you to oversee and represent us and they truly don't. Some abuse their authority and muzzle us.

We have no true freedom of speech and when we say something; try to tell these government officials and clergy members they are hurting us, they put you in jail and drum up false charges against you. You are black listed and your family members are put through hell because of these wicked and evil people.

Your life have no worth because some of them and or these wicked and evil people hide behind the coat tail of religion whilst their own brothers and sisters carry out anus crimes in the name of religion; their god and gods including idols. Now tell me, are they (these leaders) truly representing you; us, or are they taking you to hell with them?

Waging war and strife with our neighbour is not representing us. They are putting enmity between you and your neighbour and causing you to die.

How many of your children have and has died on the battlefield of death because bullies; global leaders love to war; create strife with their neighbours?

Is it necessary to fight with your neighbour constantly?

Why fight a war and or battle that do not concern you?

Thus the dream with Konshens I guess. What don't concern us as a people and nation we are to truly leave it alone. **NO ONE CAN REFORM THE DEVIL AND OR EVIL**

OUR JOURNEY/MY ANGER

<u>SO LEAVE WICKED AND EVIL PEOPLE TO THEIR OWN DEMISE; HELL AND DEATH.</u>

No government official should have to spend billions of your tax dollars on war and or disease and war machines. Every man has a right to live, but with these officials you cannot live. To them you have to go hungry and to get some food you have to be your brother's enemy. <u>Bob Marley</u>

This is wrong on our part, but yet as humans; individuals in society, we cannot see this nor can we gravitate to the truth.

No government official or clergy should have to lie to you.

Not because they are hell bound should you as the citizen of the land should be hell bound with them.

As humans; individuals, we've forgotten that <u>**NO ONE CAN MAKE YOU BELONG BECAUSE YOU ALREADY BELONG. WHEN YOU SIN AND DO ALL THAT IS WICKED AND EVIL, YOU NO LONGER BELONG TO LIFE. YOU BECOME APART OF THE CULTURE AND REALM OF DEATH. SO DEATH**</u>

BECOMES YOUR HERITAGE; FATHER AND RIGHT AND NOT LIFE.

No one had to give up their place with Lovey, but due to lies we've done this; thus billions are slated to die.

BECAUSE OF SIN, LOVEY DID WALK AWAY FROM BILLIONS OF US AND WE CANNOT RETRIEVE HIM AND OR GET HIM BACK. JUST ASK EVE AND OR EVENING. She went against Lovey and she was kicked out of his realm never to ever enter and or return again.

We've forgotten that when Lovey walk away from us it's indefinite. You cannot get back into his realm and or abode no matter how hard you try.

I'VE TOLD YOU, THE SAVING GRACE THAT IS GIVEN IS NOT FOR WICKED AND EVIL PEOPLE, IT'S FOR THE GOOD AND CLEAN; PURE AT HEART OF THIS WORLD.

LOVEY CANNOT SAVE PEOPLE THAT TRULY DO NOT BELONG TO HIM. IF YOU ARE OF THE DEVIL YOU ARE OF THE DEVIL, AND THE DEVIL MUST SAVE YOU. Thus you were told of the enmity and or strife that was put between good and evil; North and South in your so called beginning; Genesis. And for those who truly know; this go further than this. The enmity was not truly enmity in that sense.

See, when lands were scattered, remnants of the truth left Mama Africa. I've told you Africa did not give up her European own. **<u>She could not; she had to keep her ties with Europe. Think Zion for those of you who truly do not know.</u>**

Africa is loyal to Europe and stop saying I am a bleeping liar and or stupid and don't know what I am talking about. Pull up the map of the world and you will see that Africa is joined to Europe; thus Europe had to keep you in the West from Mama; Mama Africa. Look at it, who is in greater debt to death financially and sin wise?

DO YOU SEE EUROPEAN LANDS BASKING IN THE LIES OF THE DEVIL?

DO YOU SEE EUROPEAN LANDS PROMOTING THE DEVIL'S AGENDA?

NOW LOOK AT AMERICA AND HOW THEY ARE MAKING A MOCKERY AND FOOL OF THEMSELF. LOOK AT MY HOMELAND JAMAICA AND SEE HOW THEY ARE MAKING A MOCKERY AND FOOL OF THEMSELVES.

GET IT NOW?

NO. Well this explanation is the best I can do because certain things you are not to know just yet.

IN MANY WAYS EUROPE KEPT THE TRUTH AND WESTERN LANDS ABANDONED IT. I know this is not the best explanation but this is the best I can do.

We in the west promote death, invade lands, join forces with death and put ourselves in more debt than European Nations.

Look at the debt load of America, South America and the Caribbean and add up the figure.

Now look at the debt load of Africa and other European Nations combined.

Do the math.

Now do you see what I am talking about?

While the West sang and danced for the devil the East were combining their resources. THE EAST AND OR EUROPEAN NATIONS HANDED THE WEST DEATH AND THE WEST ACCEPTED.

Some lands I know did not join the European Nations financially and this is fine and good because some European lands must crumble. And I am so going to leave this right now because I am getting jumbled up. Said too much and now you kinda know some of the truth. This is the best I can do because it is hard to truly explain and now is not the right time for you; for you to know the full truth. You can put it together on an economic and spiritual level and find the truth for yourself.

Some nations in Eurasia belong to the devil; thus if they could not get into Lovey's kingdom and above THE NOW ISRAEL AND JUDAH WAS NOT GOING TO GET IN. THEY HAD TO DESTROY AMERICA AND JAMAICA; THUS ISRAEL AND JUDAH WHORED AND DID ALL THAT WAS WICKED AND EVIL IN THE EYES AND SIGHT OF GOD AND MAN. JAMAICA WAS DEEMED UNCLEAN; DIRTY BY LOVEY AND AMERICA WAS AND OR IS CLAIMED BY DEATH; THE DEVIL AND I'VE TOLD YOU THIS IN SOME OF MY OTHER BOOKS IN THE MICHELLE JEAN SERIES OF BOOKS.

Your lying holy book; bible which is the book of codes told you this. <u>God did not put strife in the hearts of man; man put war and strife; hatred in the hearts of man; humans.</u> You all followed this book (your holy bible) to a tee without knowing that this book defies Lovey; Good God and Allelujah all around. Now tell me, why would Lovey seal the truth and or hide the truth from his good and true people?

Why would he do this if he Lovey is trying to save you?

Truly think because I've told you; men are liars and all they've ever done is tell lies on the truth; Lovey. So truly woe be unto the clergy of this world globally because they will have more than hell to pay. Their punishment in hell will truly be more than they can bear for real.

<u>Thus strive not to be like them because they are sealed with the time of death 6666; WHICH IS YOUR ARMY TIME; MAN'S TIME TO DIE.</u>

I've also told you; if I am the saving grace of humanity, I will not save anyone that is wicked and evil. I refuse to because evil and wicked people know what they are doing; thus the hurt and pain they cause in this earth and in the spiritual realm. ***<u>THERE CANNOT BE ANY STRAYS OR PICKEY BACKING WHEN IT COMES TO ME BECAUSE THERE ARE NO PICKEY BACK SERVICE ALLOWED.</u>***

You chose to do evil, so continue to do evil. I will not save you because in truth, the wicked and evil of this earth; world is truly not my concern.

Michelle

OUR JOURNEY/MY ANGER

This part of the book I took from another book. Yes I am angry and I did let my anger get the best of me here.

I so want and need our people to wake up and do better. I know the hardships that is coming and if we as black people don't wake up then we are going to be left behind.

I've told you in other books that, "HELL IS FULL OF BLACK PEOPLE AND RECRUITING MORE." So if we truly don't begin to clean our dirty linen of self then truly good luck.

You now see and know that the church cannot save you. So truly save yourself if you want to live.

As for you Ninja Man; (Desmond Ballentine). I saw something December 12, 2015 and it's time you stop dicking around with life. Man yu nuh noa sey death, the death you are spewing from your mouth is your death?

Death surrounds you thus I see your death. Guard your health and truly take care of you because you truly don't know what a clock a strike you. Start eating better and cut down on the drugs you are taking. Your body cannot take it thus truly cut down. Weed can be good but it can also be your death. Read between the lines because the source is greater and what you think I don't know I truly know; see, thus weed+. You have the right talk in regards to what Jamaica need. Work wisely to help Jamaica and the Jamaican People achieve a better tomorrow. Do not just talk the talk, walk the walk. Jamaicans truly need to do better for self. Gun violence truly do not pay. You cannot praise death and have life. No one can.

No one can find life in death; all they can and will find is death; so do better.

Life is given but we as Jamaican can no longer throw it away and become like the dead. **WE ARE NOT THE CHILDREN OF JESUS; THE FIRST BEGOTTEN OF THE DEAD.**

THUS, IF JESUS IS THE FIRST BEGOTTEN OF THE DEAD; WHO IS THE FIRST BORN AND OR THE FIRST BEGOTTEN OF LIFE?

Can death give good and true life?

Can death give life?

Is death not death; dead?

So why would anyone think they can find life in death if death is dead; death?

So here we go with my tirade.

Michelle

I AM BLACK AND PROUD. PROUD OF FUCKING WHAT?

WHAT THE FUCK DO WE HAVE TO BE PROUD OF? OH, WE ARE PROUD OF BEING THE TARGET FOR MANY AND THE LAP DOGS OF THE GLOBE LITERALLY.

DON'T TALK ABOUT BLACK PRIDE IF YOU'VE GOT NONE. WE'VE DISGRACED OUR ANCESTORS; TRUE ANCESTORS INCLUDING LOVEY, SO WHAT SAY THE LOTS OF YOU; US?.

SHAMELESS AND AMBITIONLESS ARE THE LOTS OF YOU BECAUSE WE ARE NO LONGER LEADERS BUT FOLLOWERS.

People that follow and dance behind the buses and trolls of death literally. **_We praise the dead, dance around like fools and act like fools for the dead. Jouvert_**

We dress like whores
Wear the hair of the dead; death
We've become loose

Many have and has abandoned their values including kids; children; true home.

Many abandon truth; praise and worship their religious gods of lies and deceit.

Many have not a true language to call their own.

Billions have not the true and living god; life.

Many claim but truly don't know.
Many live for fashion
Ego
False hope
Lies
Deceit

Many have become the abandoned
Homeless
Dead

Some of us women have kids and expect others to support and look after them. We're all fake thus we sell self. Thus your lying holy book said; women shall have children in pain. Read between the lines and know the truth. Your eyes are open now, so truly see and more importantly know the truth of life and live life good and true.

Instead of embracing our natural self, some bleach out, wear fake hair and put down their nappy and happy as pappy natural and kinky hair.

Some become bed trolls for this man and that man including women. **So tell me, why the hell should Lovey send someone to die for people that have no shame or content of character; self respect when it comes to self?**

So don't tell me about how you are proud to be BLACK WHEN YOU DON'T KNOW THAT THE FUCK IT IS TO BE BLACK PERIOD.

Look at the black race globally and see how we are depicted. Are we not depicted as the lowest of the low?

Are we not used and abused as a race not just by others but by our own; so called own?

None one of us can see the disparity of blacks to whites; white lands and see just how disgusting our black leaders of the globe are. FUCKING SELL OUTS THAT HAVE ABSOLUTELY NO FUCKING BLACK PRIDE OR SENSE.

UNNU CALL UNNUSELF BLACK. WELL I TAKE BACK THE BLACK FOUNDATION OF LIFE FROM ALL OF YOU GLOBALLY BECAUSE NONE OF YOU DESERVE IT. YOU'RE ALL FUCKING SELL OUTS AND YOU'RE ALL FUCKING DISGRACES TO THE BLACK RACE; GOOD AND TRUE LIFE.

WORTHLESS HAVE WE BECOME THUS WORTHLESS WE STAND BEFORE GOD AND MAN.

Don't talk about creation because not one of us know about creation.

Not one of us stand up for black pride and culture; our true lineage. Go there, yes go there and tell me about Malcolm X, Martin Luther King Jr., Bob Marley, Tata Madiba (Nelson Mandela), Nanny, Paul Bogle, Marcus Mosiah Garvey, Moses, Adam and Eve of your nasty book including your fake ass son of death; Jesus. Yes come tell me mek mi cuss out unnu wawawarait tantarit claate.

NO ONE THAT IS OF LOVEY CAN TAKE RELIGION OF ANY KIND TO MAN; HUMANS. RELIGION IS DEATH; THUS ANY MESSENGER THAT COMES IN THE NAME OF RELIGION AND GIVE YOU RELIGION GIVES YOU DEATH.

ANY MESSENGER THAT COME TO YOU IN THE NAME OF LOVEY AND DO THAT WHICH HE OR SHE IS NOT TO DO; LIKE SIDE AND JOIN FORCES WITH DEATH; GIVES YOU DEATH. THEY TEETER TOTTER ON BOTH SIDES OF THE FENCE; THUS THEIR HELL AND OR HOME IS TRULY NOT LIKE YOUR HELL AND HOME. THEY WALKED IN THE VALLEY OF THE DEAD THUS THE VALLEY OF THE KINGS LITERALLY. THEY TOO MUST BE SAVED THUS THEIR RESTING PLACE IS NOT LIKE THE RESTING PLACE OF OTHERS. THEY CARRIED BOTH GOOD AND EVIL AND DID BOTH GOOD AND EVIL IN LIFE; IN THE EYES AND SIGHT OF GOD AND MAN.

Yes you are saying they must go to hell like everyone else but they cannot go to hell like everyone else. Despite their wrongs, they did give you the truth; full truth that was given to them. Not all of the above this saving grace applies to. Now take Marcus Mosiah Garvey, Nanny and

Paul Bogle out because as far as I know, they did not follow death; meaning give any of you religions of death to kill you in the living and spiritual world. I could be wrong and if I am Lovey, truly forgive me.

Take Bob Marley and Tata Madiba out because they are in the Valley of the Kings literally. And as far as I know, they have a saving grace because one was given unto them by me. I will not change this because truth is truth and truth must prevail at all cost. Yes they did wrong, but am I not guilty of wrongs too? Have I not sinned?

Their message and worth; value is there, so why would I not save them? 27 years is a long time to stay in man's earthly hell for wanting and needing what is best for your people.

*Both men, Bob and Tata did what they could for their people. All Bob had was **redemption songs** and he told you this. He did not lie to you. He delivered the message of God in his music; it was his people that could not comprehend the truth that he told. Yes he went into politics and that contributed to his downfall.*

MESSENGERS CANNOT GO INTO RELIGION AND POLITICS.

WE CAN TELL YOU ABOUT IT, BUT WE CANNOT TAKE SIDES WITH EITHER. RELIGION AND POLITICS ARE BROTHERS; DEATH AND WE CANNOT JOIN FORCES WITH DEATH PERIOD. THIS IS THE LAW AND THIS IS WHY I TELL

YOU, I WILL NOT TELL ANYONE TO CHOOSE LOVEY BECAUSE WE SHOULD KNOW BETTER. GOOD AND TRUE LIFE IS GIVEN AND WE ARE TO LIVE LIFE GOOD AND CLEAN; TRUE.

WE ARE TO CHOOSE GOOD AND TRUE LIFE AT ALL TIMES AND IF I TELL YOU TO CHOOSE LOVEY, THEN I AM TAKING AWAY YOUR FUNDAMENTAL RIGHT AND RIGHTS OF CHOICE FROM YOU AND I TRULY CANNOT DO THAT. **<u>YOUR RIGHT IS YOUR RIGHT AND IT'S UP TO YOU TO CHOOSE AND BILLIONS OF YOU DID CHOOSE DEATH OVER LIFE.</u>** *THUS THE END OF MAN; HUMANS GLOBALLY IS BEFORE 2032.*

<u>*FURTHER, I WILL NOT GET INVOLVED IN ANYONE'S POLITICS BECAUSE AS POLITICAL LEADERS GLOBALLY YOU HAVE TO FEED DEATH AND I REFUSE TO SEND ANYONE ON THE BATTLEFIELD AND FIELDS OF DEATH TO DIE.*</u> *SO I CUSS OUT THE POLITICAL LEADERS OF THE GLOBE IN ORDER FOR THEM TO DO BETTER FOR THEIR LAND AND PEOPLE. You say you are a leader, then lead truthfully; good. Your people are trusting you as a leader with their well being so take care of them; your people and don't create strife with others.*

NO ONE CAN HAVE DOMINION OVER EARTH BECAUSE EARTH BELONG TO NONE OF US.

WE WERE BORN TO EARTH AND OR IN EARTH NOT THE OTHER WAY AROUND. COME ON NOW.

EARTH WAS THERE BEFORE US; SO HOW THE HELL CAN WE LAY CLAIM TO HER?

DOES EARTH CARRY YOUR NAME OR DO YOU NOT BORROW HER NAME AND THEN TURN AROUND AND DESTROY AND KILL HER FOR WHAT TRULY AND RIGHTLY BELONGS TO HER?

SO YES I REFUSE TO JOIN THEM (RELIGION AND POLITICS) IN DEATH'S ONHOLY MATRIMONY. THUS YOU HAVE MANY LEADERS OF THE GLOBE OBSESSED WITH POWER AND CONTROL. AND BECAUSE OF THIS, THEY TREAT YOU THE CITIZENS OF THE LAND INCLUDING THE LAND UNFAIRLY.

YOU ARE OPPRESSED AND THEIR ISN'T A DAMNED THING ANY OF YOU CAN DO ABOUT IT. MANY OF YOU GIVE YOUR GOOD UP GOOD UP LIVES TO THEM AND THIS IS A DAMN SHAME. YOU CANNOT GIVE THE DEVIL AND HIS CHILDREN YOUR GOOD UP GOOD UP LIFE. LIFE; GOOD AND TRUE LIFE IS WORTH LIVING AND I KEEP TELLING YOU THIS.

Yes at times I am down on life, but life is truly worth living. At the end of the day; it is your life and not another man or woman's life. You can save you, so truly save you because at the end of the day; **<u>NO ONE DIRTY CAN SAVE YOU. ALL THEY CAN DO IS MAKE YOU DIRTY; UNCLEAN; FILTHY.</u>**

I'VE TOLD YOU TIME AND TIME AGAIN; LOVEY CANNOT COME INTO A DIRTY PLANET. SO HOW THE HELL IS HE GOING TO SAVE US IF WE AS A NATION AND PEOPLE DO NOT MAKE OURSELVES CLEAN INDIVIDUALLY?

THINK.

You are clean and your pastor is dirty. How are you clean?

Have you not taken on the dirty and filth; nastiness of your pastor?

Go back to Adam and Eve of your nasty book called the holy bible that men wrote. Did it not say Adam and Eve disobeyed and got kicked out of God's garden? So what makes you any different?

Are you not dirtying yourself like Adam and Eve?

Are you not disobeying Lovey by going into unclean and or dirty places to side with death against Lovey?

So how can Lovey save you if you are not clean; dirty?

But I need a place to worship and praise God.

So praise and worship your god in your churches because LOVEY REQUIRES NOT A CHURCH. **HE LOVEY REQUIRES A GOOD AND CLEAN; TRUE HOME.**

You cannot say you love God and trample down god; THUS I SHOULD LEAVE YOU ALONE BECAUSE YOUR GOD IS TRULY NOT LOVEY; GOOD GOD AND ALLELUJAH.

I have to realize and recognize this.

Humans are not true and it is a shame.

Going back to above; take Moses out of the equation completely and leave the rest.

But the bible said Moses killed and blood is on his hands.

And I say and tell you this.

MOSES COULD NEVER EVER KILL ANYONE AND TAKE LIFE; GOOD AND TRUE LIFE OUT OF EGYPT. IMPOSSIBLE AND FORBIDDEN ON EVERY LEVEL OF LIFE.

ABSOLUTELY NO ONE THAT HAS BLOOD ON OR IN THEIR HANDS CAN TAKE LIFE OUT OF ANY LAND OR LANDS OF GOD; LOVEY, GOOD GOD AND ALLELUJAH. NEVER GONNA HAPPEN AND WILL NEVER HAPPEN.

Know the truth because the BABYLONIANS ARE MASTER LIARS AND THEY DO LIE ON LOVEY AND HIS CHILDREN AND PEOPLE.

So all of you can bite me because not one of you deserve the black coat of armour of Lovey.

Fucking disgrace that other nations spit upon and look down upon. No wonder other races use the lots of you as fucking target practice. YOU'RE ALL FUCKING VALUELESS; HENCE YOU'RE CLASSED AS MONKEYS, COONS AND APES AMONGST OTHER THINGS.

Does not say much for us as black people does it? And say it white people because the lots of you are no fucking different. **<u>You're all a fucking disgrace to life because you walk and kill for sport, thus you're fucking cursed; was cursed by her; your own fucking white own.</u>** You talk about supremacy; white supremacy, but you're not fucking supreme; you're true death. Thus you steal other peoples;

your brothers own, land, culture, heritage, roots, wealth; den tun roune an kill dem without knowing you're killing your own fucking brother and sister. Brother killing brother without knowing it; den yu expec wi fi tun di audda cheek like nothing happen. Wi anno Jesus; your fucking dead and death.

BITCH YOU CUT DOWN AND CHOP DUNG; KILL YOUR TREE OF LIFE WITH US, DEN WANT WI FI SAVE UNNU AFTA WHA UNNU DU TO WI?

WHAT FUCKING GAUL TO RIGILE.

UNNU KILL WI
ABUSE WI
TELL LIE PAN WI
CREATE GERMS AND DISEASES FI DESTROY AN KILL WI
CALL WI DI WUSS KINE A NAME
RAPE AND RAB WI
CUSS WI
SHUN WI AND MORE

EVERY TING UNNU DU TO WI FI DESTROY AND KILL WI AND WI FI TUN ROUNE AN SAVE UNNU CLAATE?

You're death's bitches BECAUSE BABYLON TURNED YOU AGAINST YOUR FUCKING TRUE OWN. YOU ARE FROM THE SAME FUCKING FOUNDATION AS BLACK PEOPLE BUT SAY OTHERWISE. So fuck the lots of you because you're no *fucking different from the black race. YOU SELL YOUR FUCKING OWN OUT TOO; THUS MAKING YOU JUST AS DISGUSTING AND DISGRACEFUL AS THE BLACK RACE.*

So bite me bitches because you now know your fucking truth and yes your fucking hell. Soh as ole people sey, nuh betta barrel nuh betta herring. We're all the fucking same.

WHITE DEATH FIGHTING AND KILLING BLACK DEATH AND BLACK DEATH FIGHTING AND KILLING WHITE DEATH.

THEREFORE, I WANT AND NEED TO HAVE NOTHING TO DO WITH ANY OF YOU. I HAND BACK LOVEY HIS FOUNDATION OF LIFE; BLACKNESS IN GOODNESS AND IN TRUTH.

IN TRUE TRUTH, NO ONE ON EARTH DESERVES HIM OR HIS LIFE; TRUTH. YOU'RE ALL A FUCKING DISGRACE TO LIFE AND OR LOVEY PERIOD.

And no, I do not take myself out of the picture because I too have sinned just like the rest of you.

We as humans are not deserving of Lovey. He's tried time and time again and we are the ones to fail and disgrace him including me with our sins. No one is perfect you are saying. Well fuck you. We are all perfect, it's our sins and generational sins that make us imperfect. And if I am contradicting myself from another book so be it and I am truly sorry.

IT'S AMAZING HOW WE SAY WE CARE, BUT YET TURN AROUND AND FUCK UP THE LIVES OF OTHERS WITH OUR GREED AND BULLSHIT. So yes get mad and say fuck me and or you and call me all the names you want, but take a good look at your life and see who's hurting whom.

TRUTH CANNOT LIE BECAUSE TRUTH DO NOT DEAL IN LIES.

<u>LIKE I SAID, IF YOU ARE NOT TRUTHFUL IN THE BEGINNING YOU CANNOT BE TRUTHFUL IN THE END.</u>

EVERYONE MUST BEGIN WITH TRUTH THUS WHAT WE KNOW ABOUT LOVEY; GOOD GOD AND ALLELUJAH ARE ALL LIES; DECEIT.

*Open your eyes. If you truly want and need to know about Lovey. Open your door to him and talk to him. He does answer and he does speak; he rarely speaks and I've told you this. Know that you do not need anyone to speak on your behalf when it comes to him. So free yourself from the prison walls that keep you prisoner. Lies cannot save you and you all know this. You were told, "THE WAGES OF SIN IS DEATH AND **<u>TRUTH IS LIFE EVERLASTING."</u>***

You know the truth so why live otherwise?

Why keep locking yourself out of Lovey's world and or kingdom and abode?

Without churches and politics we will have a lawless society you are saying?

Are we not living in a lawless society now?

Do governments and others that work for evil here on earth not kill, write law and laws to suit and please them so that they can go on killing in the name of death?

Are there not different sets of laws outlined for the wicked and evil in this world?

Do we not live by these different sets of laws?

NOW LOOK AT IT. DID WE NOT SAY GOD HAS COMMANDMENTS AS OUTLINED BY MOSES?

Take your bible and read them in Exodus. No, Lovey won't sin you for this because I am telling you to do it to get our point across; Lovey's and mine. So no Lovey, please do not hold anyone guilty and or of sin if he or she does this.

Read the laws and or commandments of Moses.

Okay, now, do we as people, the so called clergy, so called politicians of the globe not break these laws and or commandments each and every day?

Do we not go against God; Lovey?

So how can we say we will live in law abiding societies if we break the commandments of God each and every day?

Do we not make our churches unclean and go in them?

Do we not make ourselves dirty by following the dirty and unclean law and laws of men and ignore the clean and true commandments; law and laws of life and goodness and truth?

We value not the laws of God. If we did, none of us would break them to please our own selfish needs; wants.

Tell me, what commandment of God is valued by man?

<u>**We need someone to oversee us yes; but we truly do not need dirty and unclean; power hungry, controlling and deceitful people to oversee us.**</u>

WE DO NOT NEED THEIR CONDEMNATION BECAUSE ALL WHO ARE DIRTY CONDEMN US AND SEND US STRAIGHT TO HELL.

I KEEP TELLING YOU CLEAN CANNOT BE AMONGST THE UNCLEAN. PSALMS ONE ALSO TELL YOU THIS.

Life for billions is winding down and it's up to you as an individual to save yourself. Clean yourself up.

I've told you, Lovey does not lock anyone out of his kingdom and or abode. We are the ones to lock our self out and keep him at bay; from us.

<u>**I've told you, I am not the final say in all of this. Lovey is and in truth, you are also.**</u> We were all given life; good and true life and it's now up to us to live it. <u>**YES WE NEED GOVERNANCE; THUS ELECT GOOD AND TRUE; CLEAN AND HONEST PEOPLE TO GOVERN YOU SO THAT YOU CAN CONTINUE TO LIVE.**</u>

We are living right now but not all.

We are not all living because billions have and has joined forces with death and given their lives over to death.

You can retrieve yourself from death because many things you truly did not know. They were hidden from you thus death has loopholes, but life hath none.

If you can retrieve your life from death do so because death does not play on a level playing field. All that you do for death, death owns you, your children and family.

Yes we were given choices Will, but it does not mean that we had to choose evil will.

Your will does not have to be dirty; it can be clean, and your clean will is dependent on you. So truly save yourself. The end is near and trust me in the final hour none will be saved. You left and or waited until the final hour to do something to save you. Now you are rushing to get all that you need to get done. It won't work because you had time to do all the good that you needed to do by making amends for your sins.

Those that are dead and gone cannot amend and or make amends for their sin and sins. They are in transition and or waiting for someone in life; the living to save them.

Thus death cannot save life; only life can save life.

And yes, this is one of the reasons why good and evil is side by side but it won't be for long. Good must rest and not see the evils of man and spirit. All that is evil must die; be truly no more and all that is good and clean, must live and stand forevermore forever ever without end. And Lovey, if I've explained this wrong please truly forgive me. I know you don't like the word transition and maybe rest would have been a better word.

There is no final hour in my book; so do what you need to do to clean you. I refuse the final hour because **_NO ONE SHOULD WAIT UNTIL THE LAST MINUTE TO SAVE SELF PERIOD._**

I've tried my best Lovey and I don't know if this is my last book. We will see because the year is not over yet. My dream world is calm and if I am cocky in any way with these words truly forgive me.

Yes I know where and how cockiness comes in and in truth, I was cocky in some of these words in some of these books. I know I want and need people to receive the truth and you, but hopefully you humble me from now on and not let me be so fierce. No, keep me fierce because I am a Lyon, Lyons, Lion. So fierceness is in my true DNA with you Lovey.

So as I close this book Lovey, continue to hold on to me and protect me always in goodness and truth.

Michelle

OTHER BOOKS BY MICHELLE JEAN

Blackman Redemption – The Fall of Michelle Jean
Blackman Redemption – After the Fall Apology
Blackman Redemption – World Cry – Christine Lewis
Blackman Redemption
Blackman Redemption – The Rise and Fall of Jamaica
Blackman Redemption – The War of Israel
Blackman Redemption – The Way I Speak to God
Blackman Redemption – A Little Talk With Man
Blackman Redemption – The Den of Thieves
Blackman Redemption – The Death of Jamaica
Blackman Redemption – Happy Mother's Day
Blackman Redemption – The Death of Faith
Blackman Redemption – The War of Religion
Blackman Redemption – The Death of Russia
Blackman Redemption – The Truth
Blackman Redemption – Spiritual War
Blackman Redemption – The Youths
Blackman Redemption – Black Man Where Is Your God?

The New Book of Life
The New Book of Life – A Cry For The Children
The New Book of Life – Judgement
The New Book of Life – Love Bound
The New Book of Life – Me
The New Book of Life – Life

Just One of Those Days
Book Two – Just One of Those Days
Just One of Those Days – Book Three The Way I Feel
Just One of Those Days – Book Four

The Days I Am Weak
Crazy Thoughts – My Book of Sin
Broken
Ode to Mr. Dean Fraser

A Little Little Talk
A Little Little Talk – Book Two

Prayers
My Collective
A Little Talk/A Time For Fun and Play
Simple Poems
Behind The Scars
Songs of Praise And Love

Love Bound
Love Bound – Book Two

Dedication Unto My Kids
More Talk
Saving America From A Woman's Perspective
My Collective the Other Side of Me
My Collective the Dark Side of Me
A Blessed Day
Lose To Win
My Doubtful Days – Book One

My Little Talk With God
My Little Talk With God – Book Two

A Different Mood and World – Thinking

My Nagging Day
My Nagging Day – Book Two

OUR JOURNEY/MY ANGER

Friday September 13, 2013
My True Love
It Would Be You
My Day

A Little Advice – Talk
1313, 2032, 2132 – The End of Man
Tata

MICHELLE'S BOOK BLOG – BOOKS 1 – 22

My Problem Day
A Better Way
Stay – Adultery and the Weight of Sin – Cleanliness
Message

Let's Talk
Lonely Days – Foundation
A Little Talk With Jamaica – As Long As I Live
Instructions For Death
My Lonely Thoughts
My Lonely Thoughts – Book Two
My Morning Talks – Prayers With God
What A Mess
My Little Book
A Little Word With You
My First Trip of 2015
Black Mother – Mama Africa
Islamic Thought
My California Trip January 2015
My True Devotion by Michelle – Michelle Jean
My Many Questions To God
My Talk
My Talk Book Two

My Talk Book Three – The Rise of Michelle Jean
My Talk Book Four
My Talk Book Five
My Talk Book Six
My Talk Book Seven
My Talk Book Eight – My Depression
My Talk Book Nine – Death
My Talk Book Ten – Wow
My Day – Book Two
My Talk Book Eleven – What About December?
Haven Hill
What About December – Book Two
My Talk Book Twelve – Summary and or Confusion
My Talk Book Thirteen
My Talk Book Fourteen – My Talk With God
My Talk Book Fifteen – My Talk
My Thoughts – Freedom
My Heart to Heart With Lovey – God

Letters to my song and words of praise and truth; My true and unconditional Love; Lovey, Good God and Allelujah

Caged
Why
I Don't Know But I Know